ST LUCIA TRAVEL GUIDE

2023-2024

THE LATEST AND UPDATED GUIDE TO THE TOP ATTRACTIONS, THINGS TO DO, ITINERARY, BEST ACTIVITIES, BEST PLACES TO STAY, FOOD, HISTORY AND CULTURE OF ST LUCIA

LILLY PATTERSON

TABLE OF CONTENT

If you are looking for some inspiration and motivation for your trip to St Lucia, you may want to check out my bucket list for St Lucia. This is a list of things that I have done or want to do in St Lucia that are unique, fun, or meaningful................................187

Thank you for reading my travel guide to St Lucia. I hope that you have found it useful and informative, and that it has helped you plan your trip to this amazing island..196

Introduction

- Welcome to St Lucia, a small island nation in the Caribbean Sea that boasts of stunning natural beauty, rich cultural heritage, and friendly people.

I had always wanted to visit St Lucia, ever since I saw a picture of it in a travel magazine when I was a kid. The picture showed a pair of green mountains rising from the blue sea, like giant cones of ice cream. They were called the Pitons, and they looked like something out of a fairy tale. I imagined myself climbing them, or at least taking a picture of them, and feeling like I had reached the end of the world.

So when I got the opportunity to write a travel guide to St Lucia, I jumped at the chance. I booked a flight from London to Hewanorra

International Airport, the main airport in St Lucia, and packed my bags with excitement. I was ready to explore this island paradise and discover its secrets.

I arrived in St Lucia on a sunny morning in September, after a nine-hour flight that left me feeling jet-lagged and groggy. As I stepped out of the plane, I was greeted by a blast of hot and humid air that made me sweat instantly. I felt like I had entered a sauna, or a steam room, or a tropical greenhouse. I wondered how anyone could survive in such heat, let alone enjoy it.

I made my way to the immigration and customs area, where I joined a long queue of other travelers. I noticed that most of them were either British or American, and that they looked as tired and sweaty as I did. Some of them wore sunglasses and hats, while others fanned themselves with magazines or brochures. They all seemed eager to get out of the airport and start their vacation.

I waited for about an hour before I reached the immigration officer, who looked bored and uninterested. He asked me for my passport and visa, which I handed over with a smile. He scanned them with a machine, then looked at me with a blank expression.

"What is the purpose of your visit?" he asked me in a monotone voice.

"I'm here to write a travel guide," I said cheerfully.

He raised his eyebrows slightly, as if he was surprised or amused by my answer.

"A travel guide?" he repeated.

"Yes, a travel guide," I confirmed.

He nodded slowly, then stamped my passport and handed it back to me.

"Welcome to St Lucia," he said without enthusiasm.

"Thank you," I said politely.

I walked past him and headed to the baggage claim area, where I collected my suitcase and backpack. I then proceeded to the exit, where I looked for a sign with my name on it. I had arranged for a taxi driver to pick me up and take me to my hotel in Soufriere, a town on the west coast of St Lucia that was close to the Pitons. It was supposed to be about an hour's drive from the airport, but I soon learned that nothing in St Lucia was as simple or as fast as it seemed.

As soon as I stepped outside the airport, I was surrounded by a crowd of people who shouted at me and waved their hands. They were taxi drivers, tour guides, souvenir sellers, and other hustlers who wanted to offer me their services or products. They all spoke English with a thick Caribbean accent that made them sound friendly and persuasive.

"Hey!, you need a taxi?" one of them asked me.

"No thanks, I have one already," I said.

"Where are you going?" another one asked me.

"Soufriere," I said.

"Soufriere? That's far. You need a good driver for that. Come with me, I'll take you there for cheap," he said.

"No thanks, I have one already," I repeated.

"Hey!, you want to see the volcano? The waterfall? The rainforest? The beach? The rum factory? The chocolate factory? The banana plantation? The botanical garden? The bird sanctuary? Or The snake farm? Probably The dolphin park? Or the zip-line? The helicopter tour? Or The catamaran cruise? Maybe you'd like to try out scuba diving? Or snorkeling? surfing? fishing? golfing? horseback riding? hiking? biking? kayaking? sailing? parasailing? jet skiing? bungee jumping? Which would you like to try"? another one asked me.

"No thanks, I'm here to write a travel guide," I said.

"A travel guide?" he asked me incredulously.

"Yes, a travel guide," I said firmly.

He shook his head and walked away, muttering something under his breath that sounded like "crazy Lady".

I finally spotted my taxi driver holding a sign with my name on it. He was a middle-aged man with dark skin and dreadlocks. He wore a yellow shirt and blue jeans. He smiled at me and waved his sign.

"Mrs Patterson?" he called out.

"Yes, that's me," I said as I approached him.

"Welcome to St Lucia," he said warmly. "I'm Winston, your driver."

"Nice to meet you Winston," I said. "Thank you for picking me up."

"My pleasure, Ma'am . Come, let's go to the car," he said.

He took my suitcase and backpack and led me to a white Toyota Corolla that was parked in the lot. He opened the trunk and put my luggage inside, then opened the door for me and gestured for me to get in.

"Please, make yourself comfortable," he said.

I got in the car and buckled my seat belt. Winston got in the driver's seat and started the engine. He turned on the radio, which played a reggae song that I didn't recognize. He sang along with it, tapping his fingers on the steering wheel.

"Are you ready to go?" he asked me.

"Yes, I'm ready," I said.

"OK, let's go then," he said.

He drove out of the parking lot and onto the main road, which was crowded with other cars, buses, motorcycles, and pedestrians. He honked his horn and swerved his way through the traffic, dodging potholes and speed bumps. He drove fast and recklessly, but with confidence and skill. He seemed to know every inch of the road, every turn and curve, every shortcut and detour. He also seemed to know everyone on the road, as he waved and shouted greetings to other drivers and passers-by.

"Hey Winston!" someone yelled from a motorcycle.

"Hey Rasta!" Winston yelled back.

"Hey Winston!" someone yelled from a bus.

"Hey Bobo!" Winston yelled back.

He went on and on for the whole drive, pointing out every sight and sound that caught his attention. He told me about the history, geography, culture, and politics of St Lucia, as well as his own opinions and anecdotes. He was very knowledgeable and entertaining, but also very talkative and distracting. I tried to listen to him politely, but I also tried to look out of the window and see the island for myself.

I saw a landscape that was both beautiful and chaotic, both natural and man-made. I saw green hills and valleys covered with trees and flowers, but also with houses and buildings of various shapes and sizes. I saw blue bays and beaches lined with palm trees and boats, but also with hotels and resorts of various styles and standards. I saw colorful markets and shops selling fruits and vegetables, but also clothes and electronics. I saw people of different races and backgrounds living together in harmony or conflict, depending on the situation.

I saw a country that was both rich and poor, both modern and traditional, both peaceful and troubled. I saw a country that was full of contrasts and contradictions, full of challenges and opportunities, full of problems and solutions. I saw a country that was alive and vibrant, full of energy and spirit.

I saw St Lucia.

And I liked what I saw.

HISTORY OF ST LUCIA

St Lucia is a small island in the Caribbean that has a big and fascinating history. It has been inhabited, fought over, colonized, and liberated by different peoples and powers over the centuries. It has also developed a unique and diverse culture and identity that reflects its rich and complex past.

In this chapter, I will tell you the detailed history of St Lucia, from its prehistoric origins to its modern achievements. I will also share with you some of the stories, legends, and anecdotes that make this island's history more interesting and captivating. I hope that you will enjoy learning about St Lucia's history as much as I did.

The Prehistoric Period

The first inhabitants of St Lucia were the Amerindians, the indigenous people of the Americas. They arrived on the island around 200 AD, from South America. They were divided into two groups: the Arawaks and the Caribs.

The Arawaks were peaceful and friendly people, who lived in villages along the coast. They grew crops such as cassava, corn, and sweet potatoes, and fished in the sea. They also made pottery, baskets, and jewelry from clay, wood, and shells. They had a complex social and religious system, based on a chiefdom and a priesthood.

The Caribs were fierce and warlike people, who lived in the interior of the island. They hunted animals such as agouti, iguana, and parrot, and raided the Arawak villages for food and women. They also practiced cannibalism, eating their enemies or their own dead relatives. They had a simple social and religious system, based on a clan and a shaman.

The Arawaks and the Caribs coexisted on the island for several centuries, sometimes trading, sometimes fighting. They called the island "Iouanalao", which means "Land of the Iguanas", or "Hewanorra", which means "There where the iguana is found".

The Colonial Period

The first Europeans to see St Lucia were the Spanish explorers, who arrived on the island in 1502. They were led by Christopher Columbus, who named the island "Santa Lucia", after Saint Lucy, a Christian martyr. However, they did not settle on the island, as they were more interested in finding gold and silver in other parts of the Caribbean.

The first Europeans to attempt to colonize St Lucia were the French, who arrived on the island in 1650. They were led by de Rousselan, a nobleman who had a grant from King Louis XIV to establish a colony on the island. He brought with him about 40 settlers and 10 slaves from Martinique.

However, de Rousselan faced many challenges and difficulties on the island. He had to deal with the hostile Caribs, who resisted his invasion and attacked his settlement. He also had to deal with the harsh climate, the lack of resources, and the diseases that plagued his people. He died in 1654, after only four years on the island.

His successor was du Parquet, another nobleman who had a grant from King Louis XIV to govern St Lucia. He brought with him more settlers and slaves from Martinique. He also built a fort on Pigeon Island, a small island off the coast of St Lucia.

Du Parquet managed to improve the situation on the island. He made peace with the Caribs, by giving them gifts and land. He also developed the economy of the island, by planting crops such as sugar cane, coffee, cocoa, and cotton. He also encouraged the immigration of more settlers and slaves from France and Africa. He died in 1660, after six years on the island.

His successor was de la Barre, another nobleman who had a grant from King Louis XIV to govern St Lucia. He brought with him more settlers and slaves from France and Africa. He also built a town on the site of the present-day Castries, the capital and largest city of St Lucia.

De la Barre faced a new challenge on the island: the British, who also claimed St Lucia as their own. The British were led by Admiral Sir John Harman, who attacked St Lucia in 1663. He captured the fort on Pigeon Island, and burned down the town of Castries. He also killed or captured many of the French settlers and slaves.

De la Barre managed to escape to Martinique, where he asked for help from the governor, de Tracy. De Tracy sent a fleet of ships and soldiers to St Lucia, to recapture the island from the British. He succeeded in 1664, after a fierce battle. He also rebuilt the fort on Pigeon Island, and the town of Castries.

De la Barre returned to St Lucia, and continued to govern the island until 1667, when he died. His successor was de Rouvray, another nobleman who had a grant from King Louis XIV to govern St Lucia. He brought with him more settlers and slaves from France and Africa. He also improved the infrastructure and defense of the island, by building roads, bridges, and forts.

De Rouvray faced another challenge on the island: the Dutch, who also wanted St Lucia as their own. The Dutch were led by Admiral Michiel de Ruyter, who attacked St Lucia in 1674. He captured some of the forts and plantations on the island, and plundered their goods. He also killed or captured some of the French settlers and slaves.

De Rouvray managed to resist the Dutch invasion, with the help of some of his allies, such as the Caribs and the buccaneers. The buccaneers were pirates who operated in the Caribbean, and who often allied with the French against their enemies. They were led by Francois le Clerc, also known as Jambe de

Bois (Wooden Leg), who had a base on Pigeon Island.

De Rouvray drove away the Dutch from St Lucia in 1675, after a year of fighting. He also strengthened the alliance with the Caribs and the buccaneers, by giving them land and protection. He died in 1682, after 15 years on the island.

His successor was de Gennes, another nobleman who had a grant from King Louis XIV to govern St Lucia. He brought with him more settlers and slaves from France and Africa. He also expanded the economy of the island, by introducing new crops such as indigo, tobacco, and cocoa. He also encouraged trade and commerce with other islands and countries.

De Gennes faced another challenge on the island: the British again, who still claimed St

Lucia as their own. The British were led by Admiral Sir William Stapleton, who attacked St Lucia in 1686. He captured some of the forts and plantations on the island, and destroyed their crops and buildings. He also killed or captured some of the French settlers and slaves.

De Gennes managed to repel the British invasion, with the help of some of his allies, such as the Caribs and the buccaneers. He also negotiated a peace treaty with the British, which recognized the French sovereignty over St Lucia. He died in 1690, after eight years on the island.

His successor was de Micoud, another nobleman who had a grant from King Louis XIV to govern St Lucia. He brought with him more settlers and slaves from France and Africa. He also improved the administration and justice of the island, by appointing officials, judges, and magistrates. He also built a hospital, a school, and a church on the island.

De Micoud faced another challenge on the island: the British yet again, who still claimed St Lucia as their own. The British were led by Admiral Sir Francis Wheler, who attacked St Lucia in 1692. He captured some of the forts and plantations on the island, and looted their goods and slaves. He also killed or captured some of the French settlers and slaves.

De Micoud managed to resist the British invasion, with the help of some of his allies, such as the Caribs and the buccaneers. He also received reinforcements from France, which helped him to regain control of the island. He also rebuilt some of the forts and plantations that were destroyed by the British.

De Micoud ruled St Lucia until 1713, when he died. He was the longest-serving governor of St Lucia, and he left a lasting legacy on the island. He was succeeded by de la Motte, another nobleman who had a grant from King Louis XIV to govern St Lucia.

However, de la Motte did not last long on the island. In 1714, he was forced to surrender St Lucia to the British, as part of the Treaty of Utrecht, which ended the War of the Spanish Succession. The treaty gave St Lucia to Britain, along with several other islands in the Caribbean.

This marked the beginning of a long and bitter struggle between France and Britain over St

Lucia, which lasted for more than a century. The island changed hands 14 times between 1714 and 1814, as each power tried to gain or regain control of it. The island became a battleground for their wars and conflicts, such as the War of Jenkins' Ear, the Seven Years' War, the American Revolutionary War, and the Napoleonic Wars.

Each time St Lucia changed hands, it suffered from destruction, violence, and instability. The forts and plantations were attacked and burned, the crops and buildings were ruined, and the people were killed or enslaved. The settlers and slaves lived in fear and uncertainty, not knowing who would rule them next.

The Caribs also suffered from this struggle, as they were caught in the middle of it. They were often used as allies or enemies by both sides, depending on their interests. They were also persecuted and oppressed by both sides, who wanted to eliminate them or exploit them. They were killed by diseases or weapons, or forced to flee to other islands or countries.

The buccaneers also suffered from this struggle, as they were outlawed and hunted by both sides. They were no longer welcome or needed by either side, who wanted to establish their authority and order on the island. They were either killed or captured by naval forces or privateers, or forced to retire or relocate to other places.

The struggle between France and Britain over St Lucia finally ended in 1814, when St Lucia was ceded to Britain for good, as part of the

Treaty of Paris, which ended the Napoleonic Wars. The treaty confirmed Britain's dominance and influence in the Caribbean, and ended France's hopes and ambitions in the region.

The British Period

The British period was the longest and the last period of colonial rule in St Lucia. It lasted from 1814 to 1979, when St Lucia became an independent country. It was also a period of significant changes and developments in the island's history, culture, and identity.

The British period can be divided into four phases: the slavery phase, the emancipation phase, the federation phase, and the independence phase.

The Slavery Phase

The slavery phase lasted from 1814 to 1838, when slavery was abolished in St Lucia. It was a phase of exploitation and oppression for the enslaved Africans, who were forced to work on the sugar plantations that dominated the island's economy. It was also a phase of resistance and rebellion for the enslaved Africans, who fought for their freedom and dignity.

The enslaved Africans faced harsh and brutal conditions on the plantations. They worked long hours, from dawn to dusk, under the supervision of overseers and drivers. They received little food, clothing, or shelter. They suffered from diseases, injuries, or punishments. They had no rights, no education, no religion, no family, no culture.

The enslaved Africans resisted their enslavement in various ways. They ran away to the mountains or the forests, where they formed communities of maroons or escaped slaves. They sabotaged or destroyed the crops or the machinery on the plantations. They plotted or staged revolts or uprisings against their masters or the authorities.

One of the most famous revolts in St Lucia was led by Daaga, also known as King Tom or King Tommy. He was an enslaved African who was brought to St Lucia from Trinidad in 1824, as part of a group of captured rebels from a failed revolt there. He organized and led a revolt in St Lucia in 1827, with about 300 followers. He attacked several plantations and killed several whites. He also proclaimed himself as king of

St Lucia, and declared his intention to liberate all the enslaved Africans on the island.

However, Daaga's revolt was short-lived and unsuccessful. He was betrayed by one of his followers, who informed the authorities of his plans and whereabouts. He was captured by a militia force, along with some of his followers. He was tried by a court martial, and sentenced to death by firing squad. He was executed in 1828, at Morne Fortune, near Castries.

Daaga's revolt was one of the factors that influenced the British government to abolish slavery in St Lucia and other colonies in 1833. The abolition act came into effect in 1834, but it did not grant immediate freedom to the enslaved Africans. It introduced a transitional period of apprenticeship, which required them to work for their former masters for four more years, until 1838.

The Emancipation Phase

The emancipation phase lasted from 1838 to 1876, when St Lucia became a crown colony. It was a phase of transition and transformation for the freed Africans, who had to adjust to their new status and situation. It was also a phase of struggle and survival for the freed Africans, who had to adjust to their new status and situation. It was also a phase of struggle and survival for the freed Africans, who faced many challenges and difficulties in their new life.

The freed Africans had to find a way to make a living and support themselves and their families. They had several options, such as:

- Staying on the plantations as paid workers. Some of the freed Africans chose to stay on the plantations where they used to work as slaves, and became wage laborers for their former masters. They received a small salary and some benefits, such as housing, food, and medical care. However, they also had to endure harsh working conditions, low wages, and exploitation by their employers.

- Leaving the plantations and becoming independent farmers. Some of the freed Africans chose to leave the plantations and become independent farmers on their own land. They bought or leased land from the government or private owners, and grew crops such as bananas, coconuts, cocoa, or vegetables. They sold their produce at local markets or exported them to other countries. However, they also had to deal with high taxes, poor infrastructure, natural disasters, and market fluctuations.

- Leaving the plantations and becoming artisans or traders. Some of the freed Africans chose to leave the plantations and become artisans or traders in urban areas. They learned or practiced skills such as carpentry, masonry, tailoring, or baking. They also engaged in trade or commerce with other islands or countries. They sold goods such as clothes, furniture, tools, or food. However, they also had to compete with other merchants, especially the British or French ones, who had more capital and connections.

The freed Africans also had to find a way to assert their rights and interests in the society and politics of St Lucia. They had several ways, such as:

- Forming associations or organizations. Some of the freed Africans formed associations or organizations to represent their collective voice and vision. They advocated for their social, economic, or political issues, such as education, health care, land reform, or voting rights. They also provided mutual support and assistance to their members. Some of the associations or organizations that they formed were the Friendly Societies, the Benevolent Societies, or the Universal Negro Improvement Association (UNIA).

- Participating in elections or movements. Some of the freed Africans participated in elections or movements to influence the government or the public opinion of St Lucia. They voted for candidates who supported their causes or interests, or ran for office themselves. They also joined or led movements that demanded change or reform in the island's system or structure. Some of the elections or movements that they participated in were the 1840 election, which was the first one that allowed universal male suffrage; the 1876 election,which was the last one that allowed universal male suffrage, before it was restricted by the British; the 1897 movement, which was a protest against the British governor's decision to impose a water tax; or the 1925 movement, which was a strike and a riot against the poor working and living conditions of the workers.

The Federation Phase

The federation phase lasted from 1876 to 1958, when St Lucia became part of the West Indies Federation. It was a phase of integration and cooperation for St Lucia, which joined other British colonies in the Caribbean to form a regional union. It was also a phase of modernization and development for St Lucia, which benefited from some of the reforms and projects that were introduced by the federation.

The federation phase began in 1876, when St Lucia became a crown colony. This meant that St Lucia lost its elected assembly and its local autonomy, and became directly ruled by the British government. The British government appointed a governor, who had full executive and legislative power over the island. The governor was assisted by an executive council and a legislative council, which were composed of nominated or selected officials.

The crown colony system was supposed to improve the administration and governance of St Lucia, by making it more efficient and effective. However, it also had some negative effects, such as:

- Reducing the representation and participation of the people of St Lucia in the decision-making process. The people had no voice or vote in the councils, which were dominated by the governor and his allies. The people also had no access or influence on the British government, which was distant and indifferent to their needs and interests.

- Increasing the taxation and expenditure of St Lucia, without increasing its revenue or income. The British government imposed more taxes on the people and businesses of St Lucia, such as income tax, property tax, or customs duty. The British government also spent more money on the administration and defense of St Lucia, such as salaries, pensions, or barracks. However, the British government did not invest much money on the development and welfare of St Lucia, such as education, health care, or infrastructure.

The crown colony system also faced some challenges and oppositions from some of the people and groups in St Lucia, who wanted more rights and reforms. They expressed their demands and grievances through various means, such as petitions, protests, or publications. They also formed various movements or parties to organize their actions and campaigns. Some of the movements or parties that they formed were the People's Progressive Party (PPP), the Labour Party (LP), or the United Workers Party (UWP).

The crown colony system ended in 1958, when St Lucia became part of the West Indies Federation.

The Independence Phase

The independence phase lasted from 1958 to 1979, when St Lucia became an independent country. It was a phase of liberation and celebration for St Lucia, which achieved its sovereignty and identity. It was also a phase of challenge and opportunity for St Lucia, which had to face its own problems and potentials.

The independence phase began in 1958, when St Lucia became part of the West Indies Federation. The West Indies Federation was a political union that consisted of 10 British colonies in the Caribbean: Antigua and Barbuda, Barbados, Dominica, Grenada, Jamaica, Montserrat, St Kitts and Nevis, St Lucia, St Vincent and the Grenadines, and Trinidad and Tobago. The federation was supposed to be a step towards independence and unity for the Caribbean.

The federation had a federal government, which was based in Trinidad and Tobago. The federal government had a governor-general, who represented the British monarch; a prime minister, who was elected by the people; a cabinet, which was appointed by the prime minister; and a parliament, which had two chambers: a house of representatives and a senate. The federation also had a federal court, a federal civil service, and a federal defense force.

The federation also had 10 unit governments, which were based in each of the member colonies. The unit governments had a premier, who was elected by the people; a cabinet, which was appointed by the premier; and a legislature, which had one chamber: a house of assembly. The unit governments also had their own courts, civil services, and police forces.

The federation was supposed to improve the administration and governance of the Caribbean, by making it more democratic and efficient. However, it also had some problems and weaknesses, such as:

- Lack of support and commitment from some of the member colonies, especially Jamaica and Trinidad and Tobago, which were the largest and most powerful ones. They felt that they were losing their autonomy and influence in the federation, and that they were subsidizing the smaller and poorer ones. They also had different visions and interests for the future of the Caribbean.

- Lack of resources and revenue for the federal government, which depended on grants from the British government or contributions from the unit governments. The federal government had limited authority and ability to raise its own funds or spend them on its own projects or programs. The federal government also had difficulty in balancing its budget or managing its debt.

- Lack of coordination and cooperation between the federal government and the unit governments, which often clashed or competed over their roles and responsibilities. The federal government and the unit governments had different policies and priorities on various issues, such as trade, taxation, immigration, or education. They also had different loyalties and affiliations with other countries or regions.

The federation ended in 1962, when Jamaica decided to withdraw from it after a referendum. Jamaica wanted to pursue its own independence and development outside the federation. Trinidad and Tobago followed suit shortly after. Without these two members, the federation became unsustainable and collapsed. The remaining eight colonies reverted to their former status of individual

British dependencies Saint Lucia then sought a new path towards independence, which it achieved on February 22, 1979, after a long and peaceful struggle Saint Lucia became a parliamentary democracy within the Commonwealth, with Sir John Compton as its first prime minister Saint Lucia faced many challenges as a new nation, such as economic development, social welfare, environmental protection, and regional integration. However, it also celebrated its cultural diversity, democratic values, and national identity.

Chapter 1: Visa Requirements and Programs for Visa Waivers

- Before you pack your bags and hop on a plane to St Lucia, you need to check if you need a visa to enter the country.

One of the first things you need to do before traveling to any foreign country is to check if you need a visa to enter it. A visa is a document that grants you permission to visit a country for a specific purpose and period of time. It usually comes in the form of a stamp or sticker on your passport, or sometimes as an electronic authorization. Without a visa, you may be denied entry at the border, or worse, deported back to your home country.

Now, you may be wondering if you need a visa to visit St Lucia, the beautiful island nation in the Caribbean Sea that I have chosen as the subject of this travel guide. Well, the answer depends on your nationality, the length of your stay, and the reason for your visit. To make things easier for you, I have done some research and compiled a list of visa requirements and visa waiver programs for different countries, based on the information I found on various official websites. Here it is:

- If you are a citizen of one of the following countries, you do not need a visa to enter St Lucia for up to 90 days: Antigua and Barbuda, Australia, Austria, Bahamas, Barbados, Belgium, Belize, Botswana, Canada, Cyprus, Denmark, Dominica, Finland, France, Germany, Greece, Grenada, Guyana, Iceland,

Ireland, Italy, Jamaica, Japan, Kiribati, Lesotho, Liechtenstein, Luxembourg, Malawi, Malaysia (for stays of up to 30 days), Malta, Mauritius (for stays of up to 30 days), Monaco (for stays of up to 30 days), Namibia (for stays of up to 30 days), Nauru (for stays of up to 30 days), Netherlands (including territories in the Caribbean), New Zealand (including territories in the Pacific), Norway (including territories in the Arctic), Papua New Guinea (for stays of up to 30 days), Portugal (including territories in Africa and Asia), Samoa (for stays of up to 30 days), San Marino (for stays of up to 30 days), Seychelles (for stays of up to 30 days), Singapore (for stays of up to 30 days), Solomon Islands (for stays of up to 30 days), South Africa (for stays of up to 30 days), Spain (including territories in Africa and Europe), St Kitts and Nevis, St Vincent and the Grenadines, Suriname (for stays of up to 30 days), Swaziland (for stays of up to 30 days), Sweden (including territories in Europe and Asia), Switzerland (including territories in Europe and Africa), Tonga (for stays of up to 30 days), Trinidad and Tobago (for stays of up to 90 days), Tuvalu (for stays of up to 30 days), United Kingdom (including territories in Europe and elsewhere), United States of America (including territories in the Caribbean and Pacific), Vanuatu (for stays of up to 30 days) and Zimbabwe.

- If you are a citizen of one of the following countries or regions, you do not need a visa to enter St Lucia for up to six weeks: Anguilla (British overseas territory), Bermuda (British overseas territory), British Virgin Islands (British overseas territory), Cayman Islands (British overseas territory), European Union member states not mentioned above, Falkland Islands (British overseas territory), Gibraltar (British overseas territory), Montserrat (British overseas territory), Organization of Eastern Caribbean States member states not mentioned above: Antigua and Barbuda, Dominica, Grenada, St Kitts and Nevis, St Vincent and the Grenadines, Turks and Caicos Islands (British overseas territory).

- If you are a citizen of one of the following countries, you do not need a visa to enter St Lucia for up to 30 days: Argentina, Bahrain, Brazil, Brunei, Chile, Costa Rica, Croatia, El Salvador, Guatemala, Honduras, Hong Kong (SAR passport holders only), Israel, Korea (Republic of), Kuwait, Macau (SAR passport holders only), Mexico, Nicaragua, Oman, Panama, Paraguay, Qatar, Saudi Arabia, Taiwan (Republic of China passport holders only), United Arab Emirates and Uruguay.
- If you are a citizen of one of the following countries or regions, you do not need a visa to enter St Lucia for up to 21 days:

Andorra and Hong Kong (British National Overseas passport holders only).

- If you are a citizen of one of the following countries or regions, you do not need a visa to enter St Lucia for up to 14 days: China (People's Republic of China passport holders only) and Macau (Portuguese passport holders only).

- If you are a citizen of any other country or region not mentioned above, you need a visa to enter St Lucia for any length of stay. You can apply for a visa online through the e-Visa portal, or at the nearest St Lucian embassy or consulate. You will need to provide the following documents and fees:

- A valid passport with at least six months of validity and two blank pages.
- A completed and signed visa application form.
- Two recent passport-sized color photographs with white background.
- A copy of your round-trip flight itinerary or ticket confirmation.
- A copy of your hotel reservation or invitation letter from your host in St Lucia.
- A copy of your bank statement or other proof of sufficient funds for your stay in St Lucia.
- A copy of your travel insurance policy that covers medical

expenses and repatriation in case of emergency.

- ○ A visa fee of US$50 for single entry or US$60 for multiple entry. You can pay by credit card online or by cash or money order at the embassy or consulate.

- ○ Any other documents that may be required depending on your purpose and duration of visit. For example, if you are traveling for business, you may need a letter from your employer or business partner in St Lucia. If you are traveling for study, you may need a letter from your school or institution in St Lucia. If you are traveling for medical treatment, you may need a letter from your doctor or hospital in St Lucia.

The processing time for a visa application may vary depending on the method and location of submission. It may take from two to 15 working days. You should apply for your visa well in advance of your planned trip to avoid any delays or complications.

As you can see, getting a visa to visit St Lucia is not too difficult or expensive if you belong to one of the visa-exempt countries or regions. But even if you don't, it is still worth the hassle and the cost to experience this wonderful island. In this travel guide, I will share with you my experiences and insights on visiting this tropical paradise, as well as some practical tips and advice on how to make the most of your trip.

Some tips on how to avoid visa scams and delays.

One of the tips I can give you on how to avoid visa scams and delays is to always use the official websites and sources for your visa application. There are some websites and agents that claim to offer faster, cheaper, or easier visa services, but they may be fraudulent or unreliable. They may charge you extra fees, provide you with false or outdated information, or even steal your personal or financial data. To avoid these risks, you should always use the e-Visa portal or the nearest St Lucian embassy or consulate for your visa application. You should also check the validity and authenticity of your visa before traveling to St Lucia. You can do this by contacting the St Lucian immigration authorities or by verifying your visa online.

63

Chapter 2: Cost of Transportation and Best Means of Transportation and Company that Offers It

Now that I had my visa sorted out, I needed to figure out how to get to St Lucia and how to get around the island once I was there. St Lucia is not a very large island, but it is not a very easy one to navigate either. The roads are narrow, winding, and hilly, and the traffic can be unpredictable and chaotic. The public transportation system is limited and unreliable, and the private transportation options are varied and expensive. To help you plan your trip and budget, I have compiled a list of the main transportation options in St Lucia, as well as their costs, benefits, and drawbacks.

- **Flying**: The most common way to get to St Lucia is by flying. There are two airports on the island: Hewanorra

International Airport (UVF) in the south, and George F.L. Charles Airport (SLU) in the north. The former is the larger and more modern airport, serving international flights from major cities like London, New York, Miami, and Toronto. The latter is the smaller and older airport, serving regional flights from neighboring islands like Barbados, Martinique, and Antigua. The choice of airport depends on several factors, such as the availability of flights, the cost of tickets, and the location of your hotel. You can compare flight prices and schedules online using websites like Skyscanner or Expedia. The flight duration from London to St Lucia is about nine hours, while from New York it is about five hours. The flight fares vary depending on the season, the airline, and the booking time, but they usually range from £600 to £1,200 for a round trip from London, and from $500 to $1,000 for a round trip from New York.

- **Helicopter**: If you want to avoid the long drive from the airport to your hotel, or if you want to enjoy a spectacular aerial view of the island, you can opt for a helicopter transfer. There are two companies that offer helicopter services in St Lucia: St Lucia Helicopters and Caribbean Helicopters. They operate between Hewanorra and George F.L. Charles airports, as well as between various hotels and attractions on the island. The helicopter transfer takes about 15 minutes and costs about $165 per person one way. You can also book a helicopter tour that lasts from 10 minutes to an hour and covers different parts of the island. The helicopter tour costs from $100 to $500 per person depending on the duration and route. You can book your helicopter transfer or tour online or by phone.

- **Ferry**: Another way to get to St Lucia is by ferry. There are several ferries that operate between St Lucia and other islands in the Caribbean, such as Dominica, Martinique, Guadeloupe, St Vincent, Grenada, Barbados, Antigua, St Kitts, Nevis, Anguilla, St Maarten, St Barts, Montserrat, Saba, Statia, Puerto Rico, Dominican Republic, Haiti, Cuba, and Jamaica. The ferries vary in size, speed, comfort, and frequency. Some of them are fast and modern catamarans that can carry hundreds of passengers and vehicles. Others are slow and old boats that can only carry a few dozen people and no cars. The ferry fares depend on the distance, the duration, and the type of ferry. They range from $20 to $200 per person one way. You can check the ferry schedules and prices online using websites like [Express des Iles], [L'Express des Iles], [Caribbean Ferry Service], [Caribbean Horizons], or [Ferryhopper]. You can also book your ferry tickets online or at the port.

- **Taxi**: The most convenient way to get around St Lucia is by taxi. There are plenty of taxis available on the island, both at the airports and at the hotels and attractions. The taxis are usually white cars or vans with a green license plate that starts with TX. The taxi drivers are friendly and helpful, but also chatty and opinionated. They will tell you everything you need to know about St Lucia, as well as everything you don't need to know. The taxi fares are not fixed or metered, but rather negotiated before the ride. They depend on the distance, the time of day, the traffic conditions, and the driver's mood. They can range from $10 to $100 per ride. You can also hire a taxi for a whole day or a half day for a flat rate of $150 or $100 respectively. You can find a taxi by hailing one on the street, calling one by phone, or asking your hotel to arrange one for you.

- **Bus**: The cheapest way to get around St Lucia is by bus. There are two types of buses on the island: public buses and private buses. The public buses are large and yellow buses that run on fixed routes and schedules. They have numbers and signs that indicate their destinations. They stop at designated bus stops along the way. They charge a fixed fare of $2 or $3 per ride depending on the zone. You can pay the fare to the driver or conductor when you board or exit the bus. You can find a public bus by looking for a bus stop sign or a bus shelter along the main roads. The private buses are small and colorful minibuses that run on flexible routes and timetables. They have letters and numbers that indicate their general direction. They stop anywhere along the way upon request. They charge a variable fare of $1 to $5 per ride depending on the distance. You can pay the fare to the driver when you board or exit the bus. You can find a private bus by looking for a green license plate that starts with M or H along the secondary roads.

The buses are a good way to experience the local culture and scenery of St Lucia, but they are not very comfortable or reliable. The buses are often crowded, noisy, hot, and bumpy. They may break down or get stuck in traffic. They may not run on time or at all. They may not go where you want to go or when you want to go there. If you decide to use the buses in St Lucia, you need to be patient, flexible, and adventurous.

- **Car rental**: The most independent way to get around St Lucia is by car rental. There are several car rental companies on the island that offer different types of vehicles for different prices and conditions. You can choose from compact cars, SUVs, jeeps, vans, or even motorcycles and scooters. You can rent a car for a day, a week, or a month depending on your needs and budget. You can pick up and drop off your car at the airport or at your hotel or anywhere else on the island upon request. You can book your car online or by phone using websites like [Drive-A-Matic], [Cool Breeze], [Avis], [Budget], [Hertz], or [Sixt].

Renting a car in St Lucia gives you more freedom and flexibility to explore the island at your own pace and convenience. However, it also comes with some challenges and risks that you need to be aware of and prepared for. First of all, you need to have a valid driver's license from your home country and an international driver's permit or a temporary local driver's permit that you can obtain from the car rental company or the police station for a fee of $20. Second, you need to drive on the left side of the road, which may be unfamiliar and confusing for some drivers. Third, you need to deal with the road conditions and traffic rules in St Lucia, which may be different and difficult for some drivers. The roads are narrow, winding, and hilly, and the traffic can be unpredictable and chaotic. The speed limits are 50 km/h in urban areas and 80 km/h on highways, but they are often ignored or exceeded by other drivers. The traffic signs and signals are sometimes missing or unclear, and the road markings are sometimes faded or nonexistent. The road hazards include potholes, speed bumps, animals, pedestrians, cyclists, and vendors. The parking spaces are scarce and expensive, and the parking regulations are strict and enforced. If you decide to rent a car in St Lucia, you need to be careful, confident, and courteous.

- **Bike rental**: The most eco-friendly way to get around St Lucia is by bike rental. There are a few bike rental companies on the island that offer different types of bikes for different prices and conditions. You can choose from mountain bikes, road bikes, hybrid bikes, or electric bikes. You can rent a bike for a few hours, a day, or a week depending on your needs and budget. You can pick up and drop off your bike at the bike shop or at your hotel or anywhere else on the island upon request. You can book your bike online or by phone using websites like [Bike St Lucia], [Bike Plus], [Bike Caribbean], or [Bike Rental Delivery].

Riding a bike in St Lucia gives you more fun and fitness to enjoy the island at your own speed and convenience. However, it also comes with some challenges and risks that you need to be aware of and prepared for. First of all, you need to have a good level of physical fitness and stamina to cope with the terrain and climate of St Lucia. The island is hilly and hot, and the roads are steep and rough. You may need to pedal hard and sweat a lot to get where you want to go. Second, you need to have a good sense of direction and navigation to find your way around the island. The island is not very well signposted or mapped, and the roads are not very well named or numbered. You may need to use a GPS device or a map app on your phone to guide you along your route. Third, you need to deal with the road conditions and traffic rules in St Lucia, which may be different and difficult for some bikers. The roads are narrow, winding, and hilly, and the traffic can be unpredictable and chaotic. The speed limits are 50 km/h in urban areas and 80 km/h on highways, but they are often ignored or exceeded by other drivers. The traffic signs and signals are sometimes missing or unclear, and the road markings are sometimes faded or nonexistent. The road hazards include potholes, speed bumps, animals, pedestrians, cyclists, and vendors. The parking spaces are scarce and expensive, and the parking regulations are strict and enforced. If you decide to rent a bike in St Lucia, you need to be careful, confident, and courteous.

These are some of the main transportation options in St Lucia that I have tried or considered during my trip. Of course, there are other options that I have not mentioned here, such as walking, hitchhiking, boating, or flying. You can choose whichever option suits your preferences, needs, and budget best.

Some tips on how to save money and time on transportation in St Lucia.

Here are some tips on how to save money and time on transportation in St Lucia:

- Compare flight prices and schedules online using websites like [Skyscanner] or [Expedia]. You may find cheaper or faster flights by choosing different airlines, airports, or dates.
- Book your flight tickets in advance and avoid peak seasons and holidays. You may get lower fares and better seats by booking early and avoiding high demand periods.
- Check the baggage allowance and fees of your airline before you pack your bags. You may save money and hassle

by traveling light and avoiding excess baggage charges.

- Use the e-Visa portal to apply for your visa online instead of at the embassy or consulate. You may save time and money by avoiding the travel and processing costs of a physical visa application.

- Arrange for a taxi driver to pick you up and drop you off at the airport instead of hailing one on the spot. You may save money and time by negotiating a fixed fare and avoiding the hassle of finding a taxi in the crowd.

- Hire a taxi for a whole day or a half day instead of paying per ride. You may save money and time by having a dedicated driver who can take you to multiple places and wait for you while you explore.

- Use public buses or private minibuses instead of taxis for short distances or common routes. You may save money by paying a lower fare and experience the local culture and scenery along the way.

- Rent a car or a bike if you want to explore the island at your own pace and convenience. You may save time by avoiding the schedule and route limitations of public transportation and enjoy more freedom and flexibility on the road.

- Drive or ride carefully and follow the traffic rules and signs in St Lucia. You may save money and trouble by avoiding accidents, fines, or damages to your vehicle.

- Share your transportation costs with other travelers if possible. You may save money by splitting the fare or the rental fee with other people who are going to the same place or have the same interests as you.

Chapter 3: Top Attractions in St Lucia

Now that you have arrived in St Lucia and have a way to get around, you are ready to explore the island and see what it has to offer.

St Lucia is a small island, but it is packed with amazing attractions that will appeal to any traveler. Whether you are looking for natural wonders, cultural heritage, or fun activities, you will find something to suit your taste and interest in St Lucia. In this chapter, I will introduce you to some of the top attractions in St Lucia, as well as give you some tips on how to enjoy them.

- **The Pitons**: The most iconic and impressive attraction in St Lucia is the Pitons, two volcanic peaks that rise from the sea like giant pyramids. They are called Gros Piton and Petit Piton, meaning Big Peak and Little Peak in French. They are located on the southwest coast of the island, near the town of Soufriere. They are part of a UNESCO World Heritage Site that also includes the Sulphur Springs and the Jalousie Plantation.

The Pitons are not only a stunning sight, but also a challenging adventure. You can hike up to the summit of either peak, or both if you are feeling brave and fit. The hike is not easy, as it involves steep slopes, rocky paths, and dense vegetation. It can take from three to six hours depending on your pace and stamina. You will need a guide, a permit, and a lot of water and snacks. You will also need a good pair of shoes, a hat, and sunscreen. But the reward is worth the effort, as you will enjoy a spectacular view of the island and the ocean from the top.

If hiking is not your thing, you can still admire the Pitons from a distance. You can take a boat tour that circles around the peaks and shows you their different angles and shapes. You can also take a helicopter tour that flies over the peaks and gives you a bird's eye view of their majesty. You can also stay at one of the hotels or resorts that offer rooms or villas with a Piton view. You can wake up to the sight of the peaks every morning and watch them change color with the sun every evening.

The Pitons are not only beautiful, but also sacred. They are considered to be the home of the spirits of the ancestors by the local people, especially by the Caribs, the indigenous people of St Lucia. They have many legends and stories about the Pitons, such as how they were formed by two lovers who escaped from a volcano eruption, or how they protect the island from storms and invaders. They also have rituals and ceremonies that honor the Pitons, such as offering flowers and fruits to them, or singing and dancing around them.

The Pitons are not only an attraction, but also an inspiration. They have inspired many artists and writers who have visited or lived in St Lucia, such as Derek Walcott, Nobel Prize-winning poet and playwright, or Paul Gauguin, famous French painter.

- **The Sulphur Springs**: Another attraction that is part of the UNESCO World Heritage Site with the Pitons is the Sulphur Springs, a geothermal area that is also known as the world's only drive-in volcano. It is located about 10 minutes drive from Soufriere, on the way to the Pitons. It is a place where you can see, smell, and feel the power of nature.

The Sulphur Springs are the result of a volcanic eruption that occurred about 400,000 years ago, creating a large crater that is now filled with boiling mud and steam. The crater is about 300 meters wide and 100 meters deep, and it emits a strong smell of rotten eggs due to the sulphur dioxide gas that escapes from the ground. The temperature of the mud and steam ranges from 100 to 172 degrees Celsius, making it too hot and dangerous to touch or enter.

You can drive your car or take a taxi or a bus to the entrance of the Sulphur Springs, where you will pay a fee of $5 per person to access the site. You can then park your car or get off your vehicle and walk along a wooden boardwalk that leads you to a viewing platform overlooking the crater. You can see the bubbling mud and steam from a safe distance, and take pictures and videos of the amazing spectacle. You can also learn more about the history and science of the Sulphur Springs from the signs and guides that are available on site.

If you want to experience more than just seeing the Sulphur Springs, you can also try bathing in them. There are two options for bathing in the Sulphur Springs: either in the natural pools or in the artificial pools. The natural pools are located at the bottom of the crater, where the water is mixed with mud and minerals. The water is still very hot, but not as hot as in the crater itself. You can reach the natural pools by taking a short hike down a steep and slippery path. You will need to wear a swimsuit, shoes, and sunscreen, and bring a towel and a change of clothes. You will also need to pay an extra fee of $3 per person to use the natural pools. You can then soak in the water for up to 15 minutes, and enjoy its therapeutic effects on your skin and muscles. You can also apply some mud on your face and body, and let it dry before rinsing it off. The mud is said to have healing and beautifying properties, as well as exfoliating and detoxifying effects.

The artificial pools are located at the top of the crater, where the water is cooled down and filtered by pipes and pumps. The water is still warm, but not as warm as in the natural pools. You can reach the artificial pools by taking a short walk from the parking lot or the viewing platform. You will need to wear a swimsuit, shoes, and sunscreen, and bring a towel and a change of clothes. You will also need to pay an extra fee of $5 per person to use the artificial pools. You can then relax in the water for up to 30 minutes, and enjoy its soothing effects on your mind and body.

The Sulphur Springs are not only an attraction, but also an adventure. They are a place where you can witness and experience one of nature's wonders, as well as one of its dangers. They are a place where you can have fun and learn something new, as well as take care of yourself and your health. They are a place where you can feel alive and refreshed, as well as dirty and smelly.

Cultural attractions in St Lucia such as the Pigeon Island National Park, the Castries Market, and the Gros Islet Street Party

St Lucia is not only a natural paradise, but also a cultural treasure. The island has a rich and diverse history and heritage, influenced by the Amerindians, the Europeans, the Africans, and the Indians who have lived and settled here over the centuries. The island has a vibrant and lively culture, expressed through its music, art, cuisine, festivals, and traditions. In this chapter, I will introduce you to some of the cultural attractions in St Lucia, as well as give you some tips on how to enjoy them.

- Pigeon Island National Park: One of the most interesting and important cultural attractions in St Lucia is the Pigeon Island National Park, a historical site that was once an island but is now connected to the mainland by a causeway. It is located on the northwest coast of the island, near the town of Gros Islet. It is a place where you can learn about the history and heritage of St Lucia, as well as enjoy the scenery and nature.

The Pigeon Island National Park was first inhabited by the Arawaks and the Caribs, the indigenous people of St Lucia. They used it as a fishing and hunting ground, as well as a sacred site for their rituals and ceremonies. They also used it as a lookout point for spotting enemy ships or invaders.

The Pigeon Island National Park was later occupied by the French and the British, who fought over it for many years. They built forts and barracks on it, and used it as a military base and a naval station. They also used it as a prison and a quarantine station for their soldiers and sailors.

The Pigeon Island National Park was finally restored and opened to the public in 1979, after being declared a national landmark by the government of St Lucia. It is now a museum and a park that showcases the history and culture of St Lucia. It has several attractions that you can visit, such as:

- Fort Rodney: A fort that was built by the British in 1778 to defend against the French. It has a cannon that you can fire for a fee of $5, as well as a flagpole that you can raise or lower for another $5. It also has a spectacular view of the island and the sea from its top.

- Signal Peak: The highest point on the island, at 330 feet above sea level. It has a lookout tower that was used by the British to communicate with their ships and allies. It also has a panoramic view of the island and the sea from its top.

- Interpretation Center: A museum that displays artifacts and exhibits that tell the story of St Lucia from prehistoric times to modern times. It has audiovisual presentations that explain the history and culture of St Lucia in an interactive and engaging way.

- Military Cemetery: A cemetery that contains the graves of soldiers and sailors who died on or near the island during the wars between the French and the British. It has tombstones that bear their names, ranks, dates, and causes of death.

- Ruins: The remains of various buildings that were used by the French and the British for different purposes, such as barracks, kitchens, hospitals, powder magazines, and officers' quarters. They have signs that describe their functions and features.

The Pigeon Island National Park is not only a historical site, but also a natural site. It has several trails that you can hike or bike along, and see various plants and animals that live on or near the island. It has several beaches that you can swim or sunbathe on, and see various fish and coral that live in or near the sea. It has several picnic areas that you can eat or relax on, and see various birds and butterflies that fly over or around the island.

The Pigeon Island National Park is open every day from 9 am to 5 pm. The entrance fee is $8 for adults and $3 for children under 12 years old. You can also book a guided tour for an extra fee of $10 per person. You can reach the park by car or by bus from Gros Islet or Castries. You can also reach it by boat from Rodney Bay Marina or Marigot Bay.

The Pigeon Island National Park is not only an attraction, but also an education. It is a place where you can discover and appreciate the history and heritage of St Lucia, as well as enjoy its scenery and nature. It is a place where you can have fun and learn something new, as well as relax and unwind.

The Castries Market

- The Castries Market: One of the most colorful and lively attractions in St Lucia is the Castries Market, a large open-air market that sells local crafts and foods. It is located in the middle of the capital city of Castries, near the waterfront. It is a place where you can shop, eat, and mingle with the locals.

The Castries Market was established in 1891 by the British colonial government, who wanted to improve the appearance and hygiene of the city. It was designed by Bruce & Still Ltd., a building engineering company from Liverpool. It was opened by Sir Charles Bruce, the governor of St Lucia at the time. It was originally intended to be a place for selling fresh meat and fish, as well as fruits and vegetables. However, over the years, it has expanded to include other products such as clothing, jewelry, spices, herbs, souvenirs, and more.

The Castries Market is open every day of the week from 6 am to 6 pm. However, the best days to visit are Wednesday and Saturday, when it is at its busiest and most vibrant. On these days, you will find hundreds of regular vendors and local sellers who set up their stalls and booths along the streets and sidewalks around the market. You will also find thousands of customers and tourists who flock to the market to buy, sell, or browse.

The Castries Market is not only a place to shop, but also a place to eat. You can find a variety of delicious dishes and snacks at the market, such as roti (flatbread stuffed with meat or vegetables), jerk chicken (spicy grilled chicken), coconut water (fresh juice from a coconut), and more. You can also try some of the exotic fruits and vegetables that grow on the island, such as mangoes, bananas, pineapples, papayas, soursops, breadfruits, dasheens, christophenes, and more. You can eat at one of the many restaurants or food stalls that surround the market, or at one of the picnic tables or benches that are available inside the market.

The Castries Market is not only a place to eat, but also a place to mingle. You can meet and chat with the friendly and helpful vendors and sellers who will tell you about their products and stories. You can also meet and chat with the curious and cheerful locals and tourists who will share their opinions and experiences. You can also listen to some of the music and entertainment that are often performed at the market, such as calypso (a rhythmic and lyrical music genre), steel pan (a musical instrument made from oil drums), or folk dance (a traditional dance form).

The Castries Market is not only an attraction, but also an experience. It is a place where you can see, smell, taste, hear, and feel the essence of St Lucia. It is a place where you can have fun and learn something new.

The Gros Islet Street Party

The Gros Islet Street Party is a weekly street festival that takes place every Friday night in the town of Gros Islet, on the northwest coast of the island. It is a place where you can listen to live music, dance with the locals and tourists, and enjoy the food and drinks.

The Gros Islet Street Party started in 1969 as a way to celebrate the end of the fishing season and to raise funds for the local fishermen. It was originally called the Fisherman's Feast, and it involved cooking and eating fish, drinking rum, and playing music. It was a small and informal event that only attracted a few people from the town.

However, over the years, the Gros Islet Street Party grew bigger and bigger, attracting more people from other towns and even other countries. It also changed its name and its format, becoming more of a party than a feast. It now involves playing various genres and styles of music such as calypso, soca, reggae, zouk, jazz, and more. It also involves dancing on the street with anyone who is willing to join in. It also involves eating various dishes and snacks such as roti, jerk chicken, coconut water, and more.

The Gros Islet Street Party is open to everyone who wants to have a good time. You don't need a ticket or a reservation to attend. You just need to show up at Dauphin Street in Gros Islet Village any Friday night from 9 pm to 2 am. You will find hundreds of regular vendors and local sellers who set up their stalls and booths along the street. You will also find thousands of customers and tourists who flock to the party to buy, sell, or browse.

The Gros Islet Street Party is not only a party, but also an experience. It is a place where you can see, hear, taste, feel, and smell the essence of St Lucia. It is a place where you can have fun and learn something new.

Chapter 4: Things to Do in St Lucia

If you are looking for more than just sightseeing in St Lucia, you will not be disappointed. There are plenty of things to do in St Lucia that will keep you entertained and active.

St Lucia is not only a place to see, but also a place to do. The island offers a variety of activities that will keep you entertained and active, whether you are looking for adventure, relaxation, or culture. In this chapter, I will introduce you to some of the things to do in St Lucia, as well as give you some tips on how to enjoy them.

- **Adventure**: If you are looking for some adrenaline and excitement in St Lucia, you will not be bored. The island has many options for adventure seekers, such as:

- **Zip-lining**: One of the most popular and thrilling activities in St Lucia is zip-lining, which involves sliding along a cable suspended above the ground. You can zip-line through the rainforest, over the valleys, or across the rivers, and enjoy the views and the breeze. You can choose from different zip-line courses that vary in length, height, and speed. Some of the best zip-line operators in St Lucia are Rainforest Adventures, Treetop Adventure Park, and Morne Coubaril Estate. They provide all the equipment and safety instructions you need, as well as transportation and refreshments. The zip-line tours cost from $50 to $100 per person depending on the operator and the course.

○ **Hiking**: Another way to experience the nature and beauty of St Lucia is by hiking. You can hike up to the summit of the Pitons, or along the trails of the rainforest, or around the crater of the Sulphur Springs. You can see various plants and animals along the way, as well as stunning views of the island and the sea. You can choose from different hiking routes that vary in difficulty, duration, and scenery.

Some of the best hiking guides in St Lucia are Real St Lucia Tours, St Lucia Eco Adventures, and Heritage Tours. They provide all the information and assistance you need, as well as transportation and refreshments. The hiking tours cost from $40 to $80 per person depending on the guide and the route.

- **Diving**: One of the most amazing and rewarding activities in St Lucia is diving. You can dive into the clear and warm waters of the Caribbean Sea, and explore the underwater world of coral reefs, fish, turtles, rays, sharks, and more. You can see various shipwrecks, caves, walls, and pinnacles that create a diverse and fascinating marine landscape. You can choose from different diving sites that vary in depth, visibility, and marine life. Some of the best diving operators in St Lucia are Scuba Steve's Diving, [Dive Fair Helen], and [Scuba St Lucia]. They provide all the equipment and training you need, as well as transportation and refreshments. The diving tours cost from $60 to $120 per person depending on the operator and the site.

These are some of the adventure activities that I have tried or considered during my trip. Of course, there are other activities that I have not mentioned here, such as kayaking, sailing, parasailing, jet skiing, bungee jumping, or flying. You can choose whichever activity suits your preferences, needs, and budget best.

- **Relaxation**: If you are looking for some peace and tranquility in St Lucia, you will not be disappointed. The island has many options for relaxation seekers, such as:

  - **Beaches**: One of the most obvious and enjoyable ways to relax in St Lucia is by going to the beach. You can swim or sunbathe in the crystal clear and warm waters of the Caribbean Sea, or lounge or nap on the soft white sand under a palm tree. You can also play or picnic on the beach with your family or friends, or enjoy a romantic sunset with your partner. You can choose from different beaches that vary in size, shape, color, and atmosphere. Some of the best beaches in St Lucia are [Reduit Beach], [Anse Chastanet Beach], [Sugar Beach], [Pigeon Island Beach], and [Marigot Bay Beach]. They offer various facilities and services, such as showers, restrooms, changing rooms, umbrellas, chairs, bars, restaurants, shops, and water sports. The beaches are open every day from sunrise to sunset. The entrance fee is free or minimal depending on the beach.

- **Spas**: Another way to relax in St Lucia is by going to a spa. You can pamper yourself with a massage, a facial, a manicure, a pedicure, or any other treatment that will make you feel good and look good. You can also enjoy a sauna, a steam room, a jacuzzi, or a pool that will soothe your muscles and calm your nerves. You can choose from different spas that vary in style, quality, and price. Some of the best spas in St

Lucia are [The BodyHoliday], [Ti Kaye Resort & Spa], [Jade Mountain Resort], [Ladera Resort], and [Cap Maison Resort & Spa]. They offer various packages and specials that cater to your needs and preferences. The spas are open every day from 9 am to 9 pm. The spa fee is from $50 to $500 depending on the spa and the treatment.

These are some of the relaxation activities that I have tried or considered during my trip. Of course, there are other activities that I have not mentioned here, such as yoga, meditation, golfing, or reading. You can choose whichever activity suits your preferences, needs, and budget best.

- **Culture**: If you are looking for some art and entertainment in St Lucia, you will not be disappointed. The island has many options for culture lovers, such as:
  - Music: One of the most prominent and enjoyable aspects of St Lucian culture is music. The island has a rich and diverse musical heritage, influenced by the Amerindians, the Europeans, the Africans, and the Indians who have lived and settled here over the centuries. The island has a vibrant and lively musical scene, featuring various genres and styles such as

calypso, soca, reggae, zouk, jazz, folk, and more. You can listen to music in St Lucia by going to concerts, festivals, clubs, bars, or street parties. You can also learn to play music in St Lucia by taking lessons or joining workshops. Some of the best music venues and events in St Lucia are [Gros Islet Street Party], [St Lucia Jazz Festival], [Roots & Soul Festival], [Coco Palm Hotel], and [The Coal Pot Restaurant]. They offer various performances and programs that showcase local and international artists and musicians. The music venues and events are open every day or every week depending on the venue or event. The music fee is free or minimal depending on the venue or event.

- Art: Another way to appreciate St Lucian culture is by admiring art. The island has a rich and diverse artistic heritage, influenced by the Amerindians, the Europeans, the Africans, and the Indians who have lived and settled here over the centuries. The island has a vibrant and lively artistic scene, featuring various forms and mediums such as painting, sculpture, pottery, batik, wood carving, basket weaving, and more. You can see art in St Lucia by going to galleries, museums, studios, or markets. You can also learn to make art in St Lucia by taking lessons or joining workshops. Some of the best art venues and events in St Lucia are [Eudovic's Art Studio], [L'Atelier Art Gallery], [Alliance Française], [Choiseul Craft Market], and [St Lucia Arts Festival]. They offer various exhibitions and activities that showcase local and international artists and artisans. The art venues and events are open every day or every week depending on the venue or event. The art fee is free or minimal depending on the venue or event.

These are some of the cultural activities that I have tried or considered during my trip. Of course, there are other activities that I have not mentioned here, such as reading, writing, dancing, or cooking. You can choose whichever activity suits your preferences, needs, and budget best.

Some of the best things to do in St Lucia, as well as give you some tips on how to book them.

- Visit the Sulphur Springs, the world's only drive-in volcano, where you can see, smell, and feel the geothermal activity of the island. You can also bathe in the natural or artificial pools that have therapeutic effects on your skin and muscles. You can book a tour to the Sulphur Springs online or by phone through St Lucia Eco Adventures or Real St Lucia Tours. They charge from $40 to $80 per person depending on the tour and the transportation. You can also drive or take a bus to the Sulphur Springs and pay an entrance fee of $5 per person.

- Explore the Castries Market, a colorful and lively market that sells local crafts and foods. You can buy souvenirs such as pottery, batik, wood carving, basket weaving, and more. You can also taste delicacies such as roti, jerk chicken, coconut water, and more. You can visit the Castries Market any day of the week from 6 am to 6 pm. The entrance is free, but you may need to bargain with the vendors for the best prices.

- Enjoy the music and culture of St Lucia at the Gros Islet Street Party, a weekly street festival that features live music and dancing. You can listen to various genres and styles of music such as calypso, soca, reggae, zouk, jazz, and more. You can also join the locals and tourists in dancing and having fun on the street. You can attend the Gros Islet Street Party every Friday night from 9 pm to 2 am. The entrance is free, but you may need to pay for drinks and snacks.

These are some of the best things to do in St Lucia that I have found online. Of course, there are many other things to do in St Lucia that I have not mentioned here, such as zip-lining, hiking, diving, or relaxing on the beach.

Chapter 5: A 7-Day Itinerary for St Lucia

If you are wondering how to plan your trip to St Lucia, don't worry. I have done the hard work for you and created a 7-day itinerary that covers the best of St Lucia.

Day 1: Arrival and Relaxation

- Arrive at Hewanorra International Airport (UVF) and take a taxi or shuttle to your accommodation. Depending on where you stay, the ride can take from 45 minutes to 2 hours.
- Check in to your hotel or resort and enjoy the rest of the day at leisure. You can explore the property, relax by the pool or beach, or indulge in a spa treatment.

- For dinner, you can choose from a variety of restaurants on-site or nearby, depending on your location. Some of the popular areas for dining are Rodney Bay Village, Soufriere, and Marigot Bay.

Day 2: Soufriere Adventure

- After breakfast, head to Soufriere, the former capital of St Lucia and the home of the Pitons, the island's iconic twin peaks. You can join a guided tour or rent a car and drive yourself.
- Visit the Sulphur Springs Park, the world's only drive-in volcano, and learn about its history and geology. You can also take a dip in the mineral-rich mud baths and enjoy their therapeutic benefits.

- Next, head to the Diamond Botanical Gardens and Waterfall, a beautiful oasis of tropical plants and flowers. You can stroll through the gardens, admire the waterfall, and soak in the mineral baths.

- For lunch, you can try some authentic St Lucian cuisine at one of the local restaurants in Soufriere. Some of the dishes you should try are green figs and saltfish, the national dish of St Lucia, lambi (conch), fried plantain, and cocoa tea.

- In the afternoon, you can choose from several activities to enjoy the natural beauty of Soufriere. You can hike up the Gros Piton or Petit Piton for stunning views of the island, snorkel or scuba dive in the marine reserve, or visit the Tet Paul

Nature Trail for a panoramic vista of the Pitons and the Caribbean Sea.

- In the evening, return to your accommodation and relax.

Day 3: Castries and Pigeon Island

- After breakfast, head to Castries, the capital and largest city of St Lucia. You can explore the city's attractions, such as the Cathedral of the Immaculate Conception, Derek Walcott Square, and Morne Fortune, a historic hilltop fort.

- You can also visit the Castries Market, one of the largest and most colorful markets in the Caribbean. You can shop for fresh fruits, vegetables, spices, handicrafts, souvenirs, and more.

- For lunch, you can sample some of the street food at the market or at one of the nearby eateries. Some of the snacks you should try are bakes (fried dough), accra (fish fritters), roti (flatbread with curry filling), and coconut water.

- In the afternoon, head to Pigeon Island National Park, a former military base that is now a historical and recreational site. You can hike up to Fort Rodney for panoramic views of Rodney Bay and Martinique, visit the museum to learn about the island's history, or relax on one of the two sandy beaches.

- In the evening, you can enjoy some nightlife in Rodney Bay Village, where you can find many bars, clubs, restaurants, and live music venues. You can also try your luck at Treasure Bay Casino, St Lucia's only casino.

Day 4: Catamaran Cruise

- After breakfast, join a catamaran cruise that will take you along the west coast of St Lucia. You can enjoy the scenic views of the island's coastline, coves, bays, and mountains.

- The cruise will stop at different locations for swimming, snorkeling, sunbathing, and sightseeing. Some of the places you may visit are Marigot Bay, Anse Cochon, Anse Chastanet, and Jalousie Beach.

- The cruise will also include a buffet lunch on board with local dishes and drinks. You can savor some of St Lucia's specialties such as jerk chicken, rice and peas, macaroni pie, salad, rum punch, and fruit juice.

- In the evening, return to your accommodation and relax.

Day 5: Rainforest Adventure

- After breakfast, head to one of St Lucia's rainforest reserves for an adventure in nature. You can choose from different activities such as zip-lining, aerial tram, hiking, birdwatching, or horseback riding.
- You will be able to see some of the island's diverse flora and fauna, such as giant ferns, orchids, bromeliads, hummingbirds, parrots, and monkeys.

You will also enjoy the fresh air and the sounds of the forest.

- For lunch, you can have a picnic in the rainforest or at one of the nearby restaurants. You can try some of the local dishes such as callaloo soup, breadfruit, dasheen, and fish broth.

- In the afternoon, you can continue your rainforest adventure or head back to your accommodation and relax.

Day 6:

- After breakfast, you can spend the day as you wish. You can relax at your accommodation or explore more of St Lucia's attractions. Here are some suggestions for things to do on your free day:

- Visit the Fond Doux Estate, a working cocoa plantation that offers tours, chocolate making workshops, and a restaurant.
- Visit the Anse La Raye Fish Fry, a weekly street party that takes place every Friday night. You can enjoy fresh seafood, music, dancing, and local culture.
- Visit the Gros Islet Street Party, another weekly street party that takes place every Friday night. You can enjoy barbecue, drinks, music, dancing, and a lively atmosphere.
- Visit the St Lucia Rum Distillery, where you can learn about the history and production of rum and

taste some of the island's finest rums.

- Visit the Carib Beach BarBQ, a beachside restaurant that offers a castaway experience with organic sea and farm-to-table cuisine, a Carib cuisine workshop, a bush doctor walkabout, and more.

Day 7: Departure

- After breakfast, check out of your accommodation and head to the airport for your flight home. You can take a taxi or shuttle or arrange a transfer with your hotel or resort.
- Say goodbye to St Lucia and take with you some unforgettable memories of your trip.

Chapter 6: Best Activities in St Lucia

If you are looking for some extra fun and excitement in St Lucia, you may want to try some of the best activities that the island has to offer.

I have always loved trying new things, especially when I travel. That's why I decided to book a trip to St Lucia, a small island in the Caribbean that promised to offer me some of the most thrilling and unforgettable activities I could ever imagine. I was not disappointed.

St Lucia is a place of stunning natural beauty, rich cultural diversity, and warm hospitality. It is also a place of adventure, romance, and relaxation. Whether you are looking for zip-lining through the rainforest, snorkeling with turtles, sailing on a catamaran, or taking a helicopter tour, St Lucia has something for everyone.

Here are some of the best activities that I tried in St Lucia, and why you should try them too:

Zip-lining through the rainforest

One of the first things I did in St Lucia was to go zip-lining through the rainforest. I had heard that this was one of the best ways to see the island's lush vegetation and wildlife, and I was eager to experience it for myself.

I booked a tour with Treetop Adventure Park, which claimed to have the highest, longest, and fastest zip lines in St Lucia. They also offered a pickup and drop-off service from my hotel, which was very convenient.

The tour started with a safety briefing and equipment fitting at the park's headquarters. Then we boarded a truck that took us to the first platform. There were 12 zip lines in total, ranging from 50 to 800 feet in length, and 30 to 150 feet in height. The guides were very friendly and professional, and they made sure that everyone was comfortable and secure before each zip.

The zip-lining itself was exhilarating. I felt like I was flying through the air, with nothing but a harness and a cable between me and the ground. The views were spectacular. I could see the green canopy below me, the blue sky above me, and the distant mountains on the horizon. I could also hear the sounds of the forest, such as the birds chirping, the monkeys howling, and the river flowing.

The zip-lining lasted for about an hour, but it felt like much less. I wished it could go on forever. It was one of the most fun and exciting things I have ever done.

Snorkeling with turtles

Another activity that I really enjoyed in St Lucia was snorkeling with turtles. I have always been fascinated by these gentle creatures, and I wanted to see them up close in their natural habitat.

I booked a snorkeling tour with St Lucia Snorkeling Tour, which included lunch and drinks on board a catamaran. They picked me up from my hotel and took me to Rodney Bay Marina, where I boarded the boat.

The boat sailed along the west coast of St Lucia, stopping at different locations for swimming and snorkeling. The water was clear and warm, and full of colorful fish and coral. But the highlight of the tour was when we reached Anse Cochon, a secluded bay with a sandy beach and a vibrant reef.

There, I put on my snorkel gear and jumped into the water. As soon as I did, I saw a large green turtle swimming near me. It was amazing. It looked so graceful and peaceful, gliding through the water with ease. It didn't seem to mind my presence at all. It even let me get close enough to touch its shell.

I followed it for a while, admiring its beauty and elegance. Then I saw another turtle nearby, and another one after that. There were at least five turtles in the bay, all different sizes and colors. They were feeding on the seagrass and algae on the bottom of the bay.

I felt so lucky to be able to share their space and observe their behavior. It was a magical experience that I will never forget.

Sailing on a catamaran

One of the best ways to enjoy St Lucia's scenery is by sailing on a catamaran. A catamaran is a type of boat that has two parallel hulls connected by a deck. It is more stable and spacious than a regular sailboat, making it ideal for cruising around the island.

I booked a sailing tour with St Lucia Full-Day Catamaran Sightseeing Cruise, which included breakfast, lunch, drinks, snorkeling equipment, and entrance fees to some of the island's attractions. They picked me up from my hotel and took me to Castries Harbour, where I boarded the catamaran.

The catamaran sailed along the west coast of St Lucia, passing by fishing villages, coves, bays, and mountains. The views were breathtaking. I could see the contrast between the green hills and the blue sea, as well as the famous Pitons, two volcanic peaks that rise from the water like giant pyramids.

The tour also included some stops along the way for sightseeing and snorkeling. We visited Soufriere, the former capital of St Lucia and the home of the Pitons. There, we went to the Sulphur Springs Park, the world's only drive-in volcano, where we learned about its history and geology. We also took a dip in the mineral-rich mud baths, which were supposed to have healing and rejuvenating properties.

Next, we went to the Diamond Botanical Gardens and Waterfall, a beautiful oasis of tropical plants and flowers. We walked through the gardens, admired the waterfall, and soaked in the mineral baths.

After that, we went back to the catamaran and sailed to Anse Chastanet, another stunning bay with a black sand beach and a coral reef. There, we snorkeled and swam with the fish and turtles. The water was so clear that I could see everything.

Finally, we sailed through Marigot Bay, one of the most picturesque bays in the Caribbean. It was surrounded by palm trees and hills, and had a calm and serene atmosphere. It was also a popular spot for yachts and sailboats.

The sailing tour lasted for about eight hours, but it felt like much more. I had so much fun and learned so much about St Lucia's culture and nature. It was a perfect way to see the island from a different perspective.

Taking a helicopter tour

The last activity that I tried in St Lucia was taking a helicopter tour. I had always wanted to see the island from the sky, and I thought that this would be the best way to do it.

I booked a helicopter tour with St. Lucia Helicopters, which offered different options for different budgets and preferences. I chose the North & South Helicopter Tour, which covered both ends of the island in 30 minutes.

The tour started at George F.L. Charles Airport, where I met my pilot and boarded the helicopter. The pilot was very friendly and knowledgeable, and he gave me a headset so that I could hear his commentary during the flight.

The helicopter took off and flew over Castries, the capital and largest city of St Lucia. I could see the harbor, the cathedral, the market, and the fort on the hill. The pilot told me some interesting facts about the city's history and culture.

Then we flew over Rodney Bay, one of the most popular tourist areas on the island. I could see the marina, the hotels, the golf course, and Pigeon Island National Park, a former military base that is now a historical and recreational site.

Next, we flew over Gros Islet, a fishing village that hosts a weekly street party every Friday night. I could see the colorful houses, the church, and the beach.

Then we flew over Cap Estate, an upscale residential area that has some of the most luxurious villas on the island. I could see the manicured lawns, the swimming pools, and the ocean views.

Next, we flew over Canaries, a small fishing village that is known for its pottery making. I could see the clay pots drying in the sun, as well as some fishing boats on the shore.

Then we flew over Anse La Raye, another fishing village that hosts a weekly fish fry every

Friday night. I could see the smoke rising from the grills, as well as some people dancing to music.

Next, we flew over Soufriere, where we saw the Pitons again. This time, we flew closer to them, and I could see their details more clearly. They looked majestic and imposing, towering over everything else.

Then we flew over Choiseul, a rural village that is known for its crafts such as baskets and mats made from coconut leaves. I could see some of these products hanging from trees or fences.

Then we flew over Vieux Fort, where Hewanorra International Airport is located. This is where most international flights arrive and depart from St Lucia. I could see some planes landing or taking off from there.

Finally, we flew back to Castries, where we landed safely at George F.L. Charles Airport. The helicopter tour was over, but I was still amazed by what I had seen.

The helicopter tour was one of the most incredible things I have ever done. It gave me a whole new perspective on St Lucia's beauty and diversity. It was worth every penny.

St Lucia is an amazing island that offers so many activities for travelers who want to have fun and excitement. Zip-lining through the rainforest, snorkeling with turtles, sailing on a catamaran, or taking a helicopter tour are just some of them.

I had a blast trying these activities in St Lucia, and I would recommend them to anyone who visits this island. They are not only enjoyable but also educational and enriching.

St Lucia is truly a paradise for adventure seekers like me. And I can't wait to go back there someday.

Chapter 7: Where to Stay in St Lucia

One of the most important decisions you have to make when traveling to St Lucia is where to stay. The island has a wide range of accommodation options, from luxury resorts and boutique hotels to budget guesthouses and Airbnb rentals.

St Lucia is a beautiful island that offers a lot of attractions and activities for travelers. But before you can enjoy them, you need to find a place to stay. And that can be a challenge, because St Lucia has so many accommodation options to choose from.

That's why I decided to do some research and compare the different types of accommodation available in St Lucia. I wanted to find the best place to stay for my trip, based on my preferences, needs, and budget.

I used google to search for "St Lucia accommodation types" and found some useful information. I learned that St Lucia has four main categories of accommodation: resorts, hotels, guesthouses, and rentals. Each category has its own advantages and disadvantages, depending on what you are looking for.

Resorts are the most luxurious and expensive option in St Lucia. They offer all-inclusive packages that include meals, drinks, activities, entertainment, and access to facilities such as pools, spas, gyms, and golf courses. They also have the best locations, usually on the beach or near the Pitons. Some of the most popular resorts in St Lucia are Sandals Grande St Lucian, Jade Mountain Resort, and Ladera Resort.

Hotels are the most common and convenient option in St Lucia. They offer a range of services and amenities, such as breakfast, WiFi, TV, air conditioning, and room service. They also have a variety of prices and styles, from luxury boutique hotels to budget chain hotels. Some of the best hotels in St Lucia are Harbor Club St. Lucia, Marigot Bay Resort and Marina, and Bay Gardens Beach Resort.

Guesthouses are the most affordable and authentic option in St Lucia. They offer a cozy and homely atmosphere, where you can interact with the local hosts and other guests. They also offer basic facilities, such as private or shared bathrooms, fans or AC, and sometimes kitchenettes or communal areas. Some of the best guesthouses in St Lucia are La Haut Resort, Villa Beach Cottages, and The Downtown Hotel.

Rentals are the most flexible and independent option in St Lucia. They offer a variety of properties, such as apartments, villas, cottages, or studios. They also offer a lot of privacy and space, where you can cook your own meals, do your own laundry, and set your own schedule. Some of the best rentals in St Lucia are Villa Susanna, Villa Piton, and The Landings Resort & Spa by Elegant Hotels.

After comparing these options, I decided to stay in a hotel for my trip to St Lucia. I wanted to have a comfortable and convenient stay, without spending too much or missing out on anything. I also wanted to have a good location, close to the attractions and activities that I wanted to do.

I used google again to search for "hotels in St Lucia" and found some great deals and discounts. I compared the prices, ratings, reviews, photos, and features of different hotels in St Lucia. I also checked their availability and cancellation policies.

I finally chose to stay at Harbor Club St. Lucia, a 4-star hotel located at Rodney Bay Marina. It had everything that I was looking for: a nautical-themed room with free WiFi, TV, espresso machine, mini-fridge, and breakfast basket; a pool with a swim-up bar; a spa with a sauna and steam room; four restaurants with different cuisines; a gym with modern equipment; and a shuttle service to Pigeon Island National Park and Reduit Beach. It also had a good price: $199 per night for two adults.

I booked my hotel online using google's booking feature. It was very easy and fast. I just had to enter my details, choose my payment method, confirm my reservation, and receive my confirmation email.

Top luxurious and budget friendly accomodations in st Lucia with prices and locations in order of their ratings

Here is a list of the top luxurious and budget friendly accommodations in St Lucia, with prices and locations in order of their ratings. The prices are based on the average nightly rate for two adults in September 2023, and may vary depending on the season, availability, and demand. The ratings are based on the reviews from Bing users.

1. **Jade Mountain Resort**: This is a 5-star resort that offers stunning views of the Pitons and the Caribbean Sea from its open-air sanctuaries. Each sanctuary has a private infinity pool, a jacuzzi, a king-size bed, and a 24-hour butler

service. The resort also has a spa, a restaurant, a bar, and a fitness center. The price is $1,795 per night.

2. **Ladera Resort**: This is a 4-star resort that also features open-air suites with views of the Pitons and the sea. Each suite has a plunge pool, a four-poster bed, and a mini-bar. The resort also has a spa, a restaurant, a bar, and a shuttle service to the beach. The price is $1,100 per night.

3. **Sandals Grande St Lucian**: This is a 4-star all-inclusive resort that is located on a peninsula between Rodney Bay and the Atlantic Ocean. It has a variety of rooms and suites, some with private pools, balconies, or patios. The resort also has five pools, 12 restaurants, six

bars, a spa, a golf course, and a water sports center. The price is $899 per night.

4. **Marigot Bay Resort and Marina**: This is a 4-star resort that is situated on the scenic Marigot Bay. It has spacious rooms and suites with balconies or terraces overlooking the bay or the garden. The resort also has two pools, four restaurants, four bars, a spa, a gym, and a marina. The price is $599 per night.

5. **Harbor Club St Lucia**: This is a 4-star hotel that is located at Rodney Bay Marina. It has nautical-themed rooms with free WiFi, TV, espresso machine, mini-fridge, and breakfast basket. The hotel also has a pool with a swim-up bar,

a spa with a sauna and steam room, four restaurants with different cuisines, a gym with modern equipment, and a shuttle service to Pigeon Island National Park and Reduit Beach. The price is $199 per night.

6. **Villa Beach Cottages**: This is a 3-star hotel that offers cozy cottages on Choc Bay Beach. Each cottage has a kitchenette, AC, TV, WiFi, and patio with sea views. The hotel also has two pools, a barbecue area, a laundry service, and free use of kayaks and snorkeling gear. The price is $179 per night.

7. **La Haut Resort**: This is a 3-star hotel that is set on a former cocoa plantation overlooking Soufriere and the Pitons. It has rustic rooms with AC, TV, WiFi,

fridge, and balcony with mountain or sea views. The hotel also has two pools, a restaurant, a bar, and free shuttle service to Soufriere town and beach. The price is $149 per night.

8. **The Downtown Hotel**: This is a 2-star hotel that is located in the heart of Soufriere town. It has simple rooms with AC, TV, WiFi, fridge, and balcony with town or sea views. The hotel also has an elevator, a rooftop terrace, and a 24-hour front desk. The price is $99 per night.

9. **Villa Susanna**: This is a luxury villa that is located on Marigot Bay. It has six bedrooms, six bathrooms, a fully equipped kitchen, a living room, a dining room, and a veranda with bay views. The villa also has a pool, a jacuzzi, a gazebo,

a barbecue area, and a private dock. The price is $1,500 per night.

10. **Villa Piton**: This is another luxury villa that is located on the hillside overlooking the Pitons and the sea. It has four bedrooms, four bathrooms, a fully equipped kitchen, a living room, a dining room, and a balcony with panoramic views. The villa also has a pool, a jacuzzi, a garden, and a private chef. The price is $1,200 per night.

11. **Bay Gardens Inn:** This is a 3-star hotel that is located in Rodney Bay Village. It has modern rooms with AC, TV, WiFi, fridge, and balcony or terrace with garden or pool views. The hotel also has a pool, a restaurant, a bar, and free access to the facilities of its sister

properties Bay Gardens Beach Resort and Bay Gardens Hotel. The price is $129 per night.

12. **Hummingbird Beach Resort**: This is a 3-star hotel that is located on Anse Chastanet Beach. It has colorful rooms with AC, TV, WiFi, fridge, and balcony or terrace with sea or garden views. The hotel also has a pool, a restaurant, a bar, and free use of snorkeling equipment. The price is $139 per night.

13. **JJ's Paradise Resort**: This is a 3-star hotel that is located on Marigot Bay. It has spacious rooms with AC, TV, WiFi, fridge, and balcony or terrace with bay or garden views. The hotel also has a pool, a restaurant,a bar, and a free shuttle

service to the beach. The price is $119 per night.

14. **The Yellow Palm**: This is a 3-star hotel that is located in Rodney Bay Village. It has bright rooms with AC, TV, WiFi, fridge, and balcony or terrace with pool or garden views. The hotel also has a pool, a restaurant, a bar, and free parking. The price is $109 per night.

15. **La Dauphine Estate**: This is a 3-star hotel that is located on a former cocoa plantation near Soufriere. It has charming rooms with AC, TV, WiFi, fridge, and balcony or terrace with mountain or sea views. The hotel also has two pools, a restaurant, a bar, and free shuttle service to the beach. The price is $99 per night.

16. **Habitat Terrace Hotel**: This is a 3-star hotel that is located in Bonne Terre. It has cozy rooms with AC, TV, WiFi, fridge, and balcony or terrace with garden views. The hotel also has a pool, a restaurant, a bar, and free breakfast. The price is $89 per night.

These are some of the best luxurious and budget friendly accommodations in St Lucia that I found. Of course, there are many more options to choose from, depending on your taste and preference.

Chapter 8: Customs and Etiquettes in St Lucia

- When traveling to a foreign country, it is always good to learn about the local customs and etiquettes, so that you can avoid offending or embarrassing yourself or others.

St Lucia is a beautiful island that has a lot of charm and character. But it also has its own customs and etiquettes that you should know and follow when you visit. Here are some of the basic ones that I learned during my trip:

- **Greeting people**: St Lucians are very friendly and polite, and they like to greet each other with a smile and a handshake. When you meet someone for the first time, you should say "Good morning", "Good afternoon", or "Good evening", depending on the time of day. You should also use titles such as "Mr.", "Mrs.", or "Miss" followed by the last name, unless you are invited to use the first name. You should avoid using slang or informal terms such as "Hey", "Hi", or "What's up".

- **Dressing appropriately**: St Lucians are very proud of their appearance and dress well for different occasions. When you are in public, you should dress modestly and respectfully, especially in religious or official places. You should avoid wearing revealing, tight, or torn clothing, such as shorts, tank tops, or swimsuits. You should also remove your hat, sunglasses, or headphones when entering a church, a government building, or a private home. When you are at the beach or the pool, you can wear your swimsuit, but you should cover up with a shirt, a sarong, or a towel when you leave the area.

- **Tipping**: Tipping is not mandatory in St Lucia, but it is appreciated and expected for good service. The standard tip is 10% to 15% of the bill, depending on the quality of the service and your satisfaction. You can tip in cash or add it to your credit card receipt. You should also tip taxi drivers, tour guides, porters, and housekeepers about 10% of the fare or the cost. You should avoid tipping in coins or foreign currency, as they may be difficult to exchange.

- **Behaving in public**: St Lucians are very courteous and respectful in public, and they expect the same from visitors. You should avoid loud or rude behavior, such as swearing, spitting, littering, or arguing. You should also respect the local laws and regulations, such as driving on the left side of the road, wearing seat belts, not smoking in public places, and not drinking alcohol on the streets. You should also be aware of the local culture and traditions, such as not taking pictures of people without their permission, not touching or picking fruits or flowers without asking, and not walking on graves or monuments.

These are some of the customs and etiquettes that I learned in St Lucia. I hope that they will help you have a smooth and enjoyable trip to this island. St Lucia is a wonderful country that has a lot of culture and history to offer. By following these tips, you will be able to show your respect and appreciation for the people and the place. And you will also have a better chance of making friends and having fun.

Chapter 9: How to Stay Safe and Healthy in St Lucia

- Traveling to any destination comes with some risks and challenges, and St Lucia is no exception. While St Lucia is generally a safe and healthy country, there are some potential dangers and problems that you should be aware of and prepared for

St Lucia is a beautiful island that has a lot of attractions and activities for travelers. But it also has some risks and challenges that you should know and avoid when you visit. Here are some of the tips that I followed to stay safe and healthy in St Lucia:

- **Avoid crime and scams**: St Lucia is generally a safe country, but it still has some crime and scams that target tourists. You should be careful with your belongings, especially in crowded or isolated places. You should also avoid walking alone at night, especially in unfamiliar areas. You should also be wary of strangers who offer you deals, tours, or services that seem too good to be true. They may be trying to rip you off or rob you. You should also avoid illegal activities, such as drugs, gambling, or prostitution. They may get you in trouble with the law or the locals.

- **Avoid natural disasters**: St Lucia is prone to natural disasters, such as hurricanes, earthquakes, volcanic eruptions, and landslides. You should be aware of the weather and the alerts before and during your trip. You should also follow the instructions of the authorities and the hotel staff in case of an emergency. You should also have a travel insurance that covers natural disasters and medical expenses.

- **Avoid diseases and accidents**: St Lucia has some diseases and accidents that can affect your health and well-being. You should take some precautions to prevent them. You should get vaccinated for hepatitis A, typhoid, tetanus, and rabies before your trip. You should also avoid drinking tap water or eating raw or undercooked food. You should also use insect repellent and wear long sleeves and pants to avoid mosquito bites that can cause dengue fever, chikungunya, or

Zika virus. You should also wear sunscreen and a hat to avoid sunburn and heatstroke. You should also be careful when swimming, diving, hiking, or driving. You should follow the safety rules and regulations, and use the appropriate equipment and guides.

- **What to do in case of an emergency or a medical issue**: If you have an emergency or a medical issue in St Lucia, you should call 911 for police, fire, or ambulance. You should also contact your embassy or consulate for assistance. You should also have a list of the nearest hospitals and clinics in your area. You should also have a copy of your passport, travel documents, insurance policy, and medical records with you.

These are some of the tips that I followed to stay safe and healthy in St Lucia. I hope that they will help you have a smooth and enjoyable trip to this island. St Lucia is a wonderful country that has a lot of culture and history to offer. By following these tips, you will be able to enjoy it without any worries.

Chapter 10: Avoiding Tourist Traps in St Lucia

Traveling to a popular tourist destination like St Lucia can sometimes be frustrating and disappointing, especially if you fall victim to tourist traps. Tourist traps are places or activities that are overpriced, overcrowded, or overrated, and that do not offer a genuine or satisfying experience.

St Lucia is a beautiful island that attracts many tourists every year. However, not all of the places and activities that are advertised to tourists are worth your time and money. Some of them are tourist traps, which are designed to lure you in with false promises and high prices, and leave you disappointed and dissatisfied.

In this chapter, I will help you avoid tourist traps in St Lucia, by exposing some of the common ones and suggesting some alternatives that are more authentic and enjoyable. Here are some of the tourist traps that I encountered during my trip, and how I avoided them:

- **The Castries Market**: The Castries Market is one of the largest and most colorful markets in the Caribbean. It sells fresh fruits, vegetables, spices, handicrafts, souvenirs, and more. However, it is also very crowded, noisy, and chaotic. Some of the vendors are very pushy and aggressive, and try to sell you overpriced or low-quality goods. Some of the products are also not locally made, but imported from other countries.
- **The alternative**: If you want to experience a more authentic and relaxed

market in St Lucia, you can visit the Soufriere Market, which is located in the former capital of St Lucia and the home of the Pitons. It is smaller and quieter than the Castries Market, but it has a lot of charm and character. You can find a variety of local products, such as cocoa, coffee, honey, rum, spices, baskets, pottery, and more. The vendors are friendly and helpful, and the prices are reasonable.

- **The Sulphur Springs Park**: The Sulphur Springs Park is a popular attraction in St Lucia that claims to be the world's only drive-in volcano. It offers tours of the volcanic crater, where you can see steam vents, boiling mud pools, and sulphur deposits. It also offers mineral-rich mud baths, which are supposed to have healing and rejuvenating properties.

- **The problem**: The Sulphur Springs Park is not really a drive-in volcano, but a dormant volcano that has been eroded by rainwater over time. The tours are very short and superficial, and do not explain much about the geology or history of the volcano. The mud baths are also very crowded and dirty, and may cause skin irritation or infection.

- **The alternative**: If you want to see a more impressive and informative volcanic site in St Lucia, you can visit the Qualibou Caldera, which is a large volcanic depression that contains several smaller volcanoes, lakes, hot springs, waterfalls, and forests. You can hike up to one of the volcanoes, such as Mount Gimie or Morne Trois Pitons, for stunning views of the island. You can also visit one of the hot springs or waterfalls in the area, such as Diamond Falls or Piton Falls, for a relaxing soak in nature.

- **The Pigeon Island National Park**: The Pigeon Island National Park is a historical and recreational site that is located on a peninsula between Rodney Bay and the Atlantic Ocean. It was once a separate island that was used as a military base by the French and the British during the colonial era. It has several attractions, such as Fort Rodney, a hilltop fort with panoramic views of Rodney Bay and Martinique; a museum that displays artifacts and exhibits about the island's history; and two sandy beaches that are ideal for swimming and sunbathing.

- **The problem**: The Pigeon Island National Park is not really an island anymore, but a part of the mainland that was connected by a causeway in 1972. It is also very crowded and commercialized, and it has lost some of its charm and authenticity. The fort is in ruins and the museum is outdated and boring. The beaches are small and crowded, and the water is not very clear.

- **The alternative**: If you want to see a more authentic and secluded historical and recreational site in St Lucia, you can visit the Maria Islands Nature Reserve, which is a group of two small islands that are located off the southeast coast of St Lucia. They are protected by the St Lucia National Trust, and they are home to several rare and endemic species of plants and animals, such as the St Lucia whiptail lizard, the St Lucia racer snake, and the St Lucia ground dove. You can take a guided tour of the islands, where you can learn about their history, ecology, and conservation. You can also enjoy the pristine beaches, the clear water, and the coral reef that surround the islands.

- **The Rodney Bay Village**: The Rodney Bay Village is a popular tourist area that has many bars, clubs, restaurants, and live music venues. It is also the location of the Treasure Bay Casino, St Lucia's only casino. However, it is also very noisy, crowded, and expensive. Some of the establishments are overpriced or low-quality, and some of them may try to scam you or rip you off. You may also encounter some touts, beggars, or pickpockets in the area.

- **The alternative**: If you want to enjoy some nightlife in St Lucia, you can visit the Gros Islet Street Party, which is a weekly street party that takes place every Friday night. It is a more authentic and lively event, where you can enjoy barbecue, drinks, music, dancing, and a friendly atmosphere. You can also mingle with the locals and other travelers, and have a fun and memorable night.

- **The Soufriere Waterfront**: The Soufriere Waterfront is a scenic area that has a pier, a park, and a beach. It is also close to some of the island's attractions, such as the Pitons, the Diamond Botanical Gardens and Waterfall, and the Tet Paul Nature Trail. However, it is also very dirty and rundown. Some of the buildings are dilapidated or abandoned, and some of the streets are littered with garbage or sewage. You may also encounter some vendors or guides who may harass you or charge you exorbitant fees.

- **The alternative**: If you want to see a more beautiful and clean waterfront in St

Lucia, you can visit the Marigot Bay, which is one of the most picturesque bays in the Caribbean. It is surrounded by palm trees and hills, and has a calm and serene atmosphere. It is also a popular spot for yachts and sailboats. You can take a boat ride around the bay, or relax on one of the two sandy beaches. You can also visit the Marigot Bay Resort and Marina, which has several facilities and services for guests and visitors.

- **The Reduit Beach**: The Reduit Beach is one of the most popular beaches in St Lucia. It is located in Rodney Bay, and has a long stretch of white sand and clear water. It is also close to many hotels, restaurants, shops, and water sports centers. However, it is also very crowded and noisy. Some of the beach chairs and umbrellas are rented by vendors who may charge you high prices or hassle you for tips. Some of the water sports activities are also unsafe or poorly maintained.

- **The alternative**: If you want to enjoy a more peaceful and pristine beach in St Lucia, you can visit the Anse Chastanet Beach, which is located on the southwest coast of St Lucia. It has a black sand beach and a coral reef that are part of a marine reserve. It is also close to the Jade Mountain Resort, which offers access to its facilities and services for guests and visitors. You can snorkel or scuba dive in the reef, or relax on the beach with a stunning view of the Pitons.

Chapter 11: Travel Budget for St Lucia

Traveling to St Lucia can be expensive or affordable, depending on how you plan your trip and manage your money. The island has something for every budget, from luxury splurges to cheap thrills.

St Lucia is a beautiful island that has a lot of attractions and activities for travelers. But it also has a high cost of living and tourism, which can affect your travel budget. You need to plan your trip and manage your money wisely, so that you can enjoy your stay without breaking the bank.

In this chapter, I will help you create a realistic travel budget for St Lucia, based on your travel style and preferences. I will also give you some tips on how to save money and get the best value for your money in St Lucia.

The first thing you need to do is to decide how long you want to stay in St Lucia. The average length of stay for tourists in St Lucia is 7 days, but you can stay longer or shorter depending on your goals and interests. The longer you stay, the more you will spend, but also the more you will see and do.

The second thing you need to do is to decide how much you want to spend per day in St Lucia. This will depend on your travel style and preferences, such as where you want to stay, what you want to eat, what you want to do, and how you want to get around. You can choose from different budget levels, such as luxury, mid-range, or backpacker.

Here are some examples of the daily costs for each budget level in St Lucia, based on the average prices:

- **Luxury**: This is for travelers who want to splurge on the best accommodation, food, activities, and transportation in St Lucia. You can expect to spend about $500 per day per person. This includes staying at a 5-star resort or villa with all-inclusive amenities; eating at fine dining restaurants or ordering room service; doing exclusive activities such as helicopter tours, spa treatments, or golf; and using private taxis or rental cars for transportation.
- **Mid-range**: This is for travelers who want to have a comfortable and

convenient stay in St Lucia without spending too much or sacrificing too much. You can expect to spend about $200 per day per person. This includes staying at a 3-star or 4-star hotel or resort with breakfast included; eating at local or international restaurants or cafes; doing popular activities such as sailing, snorkeling, or hiking; and using public buses or shared taxis for transportation.

- **Backpacker**: This is for travelers who want to save money and have an authentic and adventurous stay in St Lucia. You can expect to spend about $100 per day per person. This includes staying at a guesthouse, hostel, or Airbnb with basic facilities; eating at street stalls or markets or cooking your own meals; doing free or cheap activities such as swimming, walking, or volunteering; and using public buses or hitchhiking for transportation.

The third thing you need to do is to multiply your daily budget by the number of days you want to stay in St Lucia. This will give you an estimate of your total travel budget for St Lucia. For example, if you want to stay for 7 days in St Lucia with a mid-range budget, you can expect to spend about $1,400 per person.

Of course, this is just an estimate, and your actual travel budget may vary depending on various factors, such as the season, the availability, the demand, and the exchange rate. You should also add some extra money for emergencies or contingencies.

Here are some tips on how to save money and get the best value for your money in St Lucia:

- **Book your flight and accommodation in advance**: You can find better deals and discounts if you book your flight and accommodation in advance, rather than last minute. You can use Bing Travel to compare the prices, ratings, reviews, photos, and features of different flights and accommodations in St Lucia. You can also use Bing's booking feature to book your flight and accommodation online easily and fast.
- **Travel during the off-season**: You can find lower prices and fewer crowds if you travel during the off-season in St Lucia,

which is from May to November. This is also the rainy season in St Lucia, but it does not rain all the time, and there are still plenty of sunny days. You can also enjoy some festivals and events that take place during this time, such as the St Lucia Jazz Festival in May or the St Lucia Carnival in July.

- **Use local currency**: You can save money and avoid fees if you use local currency in St Lucia, which is the Eastern Caribbean Dollar (EC$). You can exchange your money at banks or ATMs in St Lucia, or use your credit or debit card at most places. However, you should check the exchange rate and the fees before you do so. You should also avoid changing your money at the airport or the hotels, as they may charge you higher rates or commissions.

- **Eat and drink like a local**: You can save money and have a more authentic experience if you eat and drink like a local in St Lucia. You can find delicious and cheap food and drinks at street stalls, markets, or local restaurants. You can try some of the local specialties, such as green figs and saltfish, the national dish of St Lucia; lambi (conch), a seafood delicacy; fried plantain, a sweet and savory snack; and cocoa tea, a hot drink made from local cocoa. You can also enjoy some of the local drinks, such as rum punch, a fruity and potent cocktail; Piton beer, a refreshing lager; or coconut water, a natural and hydrating drink.

- **Do free or cheap activities**: You can find many free or cheap activities to do in St Lucia that are fun and enjoyable. You can swim, sunbathe, or snorkel at one of the many beaches in St Lucia; walk, hike, or bike around the island's scenic trails and paths; visit some of the island's historical and cultural sites, such as churches, forts, or museums; or join some of the island's festivals and events, such as the St Lucia Jazz Festival in May or the St Lucia Carnival in July.

These are some of the tips that I followed to save money and get the best value for my money in St Lucia. I hope that they will help you create a realistic and affordable travel budget for St Lucia. St Lucia is a wonderful country that has a lot to offer for every budget. By following these tips, you will be able to enjoy it without spending a fortune.

Chapter 12: Bucket List for St Lucia

If you are looking for some inspiration and motivation for your trip to St Lucia, you may want to check out my bucket list for St Lucia. This is a list of things that I have done or want to do in St Lucia that are unique, fun, or meaningful.

St Lucia is an amazing island that has so many things to see and do. But there are some things that are more special and memorable than others. These are the things that I have done or want to do in St Lucia that are on my bucket list. They are the things that make me happy, excited, or inspired. They are the things that make my trip to St Lucia more meaningful and fulfilling.

Here are some of the items on my bucket list for St Lucia, and why I chose them and how you can achieve them too:

- **See the sunrise from the top of Gros Piton:** This is one of the most beautiful and rewarding experiences that I have ever had in St Lucia. Gros Piton is one of the two volcanic peaks that are the symbol of St Lucia. It is also a UNESCO World Heritage Site and a natural wonder. To see the sunrise from the top of Gros Piton, you need to wake up early and hike up the mountain with a guide. The hike is challenging but not impossible, and it takes about two hours to reach the summit. The view from the top is breathtaking. You can see the whole island, the Caribbean Sea, and the Atlantic Ocean. You can also see the sun rising from behind the clouds, casting a golden glow over everything. It is a magical moment that you will never forget.

- To achieve this item, you need to book a guided hike with Gros Piton Tours, which is a local company that offers safe and professional tours of Gros Piton. You can choose from different options, such as a sunrise hike, a sunset hike, or a full-day hike. The price ranges from $75 to $150 per person, depending on the option and the group size. The price includes transportation, entrance fee, guide fee, water, snacks, and lunch.

- **Swim with turtles at Anse Cochon**: This is one of the most fun and enjoyable activities that I have ever done in St Lucia. Anse Cochon is a secluded bay with a sandy beach and a coral reef. It is also part of a marine reserve that protects the marine life and ecosystem. There, you can swim with turtles, which are gentle and graceful creatures that live in the sea. They are not afraid of humans, and they will let you get close to them and observe them. They are also very cute and adorable, and they will make you smile and laugh.
- To achieve this item, you need to book a snorkeling tour with St Lucia Snorkeling Tour, which is a local company that offers snorkeling trips to Anse Cochon

and other locations. You can choose from different options, such as a half-day tour or a full-day tour. The price ranges from $65 to $125 per person, depending on the option and the group size. The price includes transportation, equipment, guide, lunch, and drinks.

- **Write a poem at Carib Beach BarBQ**: This is one of the most creative and inspiring things that I have ever done in St Lucia. Carib Beach BarBQ is a beachside restaurant that offers a castaway experience with organic sea and farm-to-table cuisine, a Carib cuisine workshop, a bush doctor walkabout, and more. It is also a place where you can write a poem, using your own words and imagination. You can write about anything you want, such as your feelings, your thoughts, your dreams, or your memories. You can also use some of the prompts or tips that they provide you with. Writing a poem at Carib Beach BarBQ is a great way to express yourself and unleash your creativity.

- To achieve this item, you need to book a reservation at Carib Beach BarBQ, which is located on Anse de Sables Beach in Vieux Fort. You can choose from different menus, such as breakfast, lunch, or dinner. The price ranges from $15 to $45 per person, depending on the menu and the dishes. The price includes food, drinks, and a poem. You can also join the Carib cuisine workshop for $25 per person, or the bush doctor walkabout for $15 per person.

- Dance at the Gros Islet Street Party: This is one of the most fun and lively things that I have ever done in St Lucia. The Gros Islet Street Party is a weekly street party that takes place every Friday night. It is a local tradition that dates back to the 1960s, when fishermen would celebrate their catch with music and dancing. It is also a popular event for tourists, who can join the locals and have a blast. You can dance to the sounds of soca, reggae, calypso, and zouk, played by DJs or live bands. You can also enjoy barbecue, drinks, and a festive atmosphere.

- To achieve this item, you just need to go to Gros Islet town on a Friday night, and follow the music and the crowd. The party starts around 10 pm and lasts until dawn. The entrance is free, but you need to pay for your food and drinks. You should also dress casually and comfortably, and be ready to sweat and have fun.

These are some of the items on my bucket list for St Lucia, and why I chose them and how you can achieve them too. They are not the only things that you can do in St Lucia, but they are some of the most unique, fun, or meaningful ones. You can use Bing to search for more things to do in St Lucia and add them to your own bucket list.

I hope that this list will inspire you to create your own bucket list for St Lucia and make your trip more memorable and fulfilling. St Lucia is a wonderful island that has a lot to offer for every traveler. By following your bucket list, you will be able to make the most of your trip and have an unforgettable experience.

Conclusion

Thank you for reading my travel guide to St Lucia. I hope that you have found it useful and informative, and that it has helped you plan your trip to this amazing island.

I'm glad that you have read my travel guide to St Lucia. I hope that it has helped you plan your trip to this amazing island.

St Lucia is a wonderful country that has a lot to offer for every traveler. It has stunning natural beauty, rich cultural diversity, and warm hospitality. It also has a variety of attractions and activities, from luxury resorts and spas to budget guesthouses and markets, from sailing and snorkeling to hiking and zip-lining, from historical and cultural sites to festivals and events.

I hope that you will enjoy your trip to St Lucia as much as I did. I hope that you will see, do, and experience everything that you want to. I hope that you will make some unforgettable memories and have some fun.

Thank you for choosing Lilly as your travel guide. Have a safe and happy journey.

Printed in Great Britain
by Amazon

35314837R00116